Present
Penguin way

Kevin McAlpin

John Van Maurik

Rock-Hill Publishing

First published in Great Britain in February 2007 by Rock-Hill Publishing

Rock-Hill Publishing
Central House
4 Roborough Walk
Hornchurch
Essex
RM12 6QJ

A catalogue record for this book is available from the British Library

ISBN (10):   0-9552588-1-2
ISBN (13):   978-0-9552588-1-7

Illustrations by Tony Healey www.th-illustration.co.uk

Edited by Michael Millar

Typeset by S. Fairgrieve, Edinburgh

Printed and bound in the UK by Thomson Litho, East Kilbride

without whom this book would not have been written

KEVIN WOULD LIKE TO THANK

Mum, Dad and Julie, Victoria, Nicholas, Anneliese and Olivia for all their support and for all the normal things. Specifically for their ideas, suggestions and knowledge: Sue White, Peter Watts, Martin Guy and Dawn Wilkinson. For their feedback, challenge and opinions: Andrew Daley, Louise Bradshaw and all the Executive Coaches from Performance Coaching International especially Gary Bean, Tammy Tawadros and Ann Kennedy. Alison McBride for naming Misha, finally Pauline from Rock-Hill publishing for believing in the idea and keeping our writing on track.

JOHN WOULD LIKE TO THANK

I would like to thank my wife Sheila for putting up with me all the times I shut myself away to write and in addition to thank all those whom I have both trained and coached over the years – I've learnt a lot from you!

about the authors:

KEVIN MCALPIN

Kevin is regarded by many as one of the UK's leading Executive Performance Coaches. Originally a highly successful sales and operational manager, Kevin has held various HR board level roles within the financial services sector.
He is a Leadership Development Specialist delivering one-on-one and group sessions to senior executives from major companies in the UK, Europe and the US. He has won many business awards by way of recognition for his innovative business-focused learning and development strategies including an Individual National Training Award. He was also a finalist in HR Manager of the Year run by the *Personnel Today* magazine. His qualifications include a MSC in HR Consultancy and another in International HRM. A certified Trainer of NLP, he is currently studying for a professional doctorate at Oxford Brookes University in Performance Coaching.

He is also a professional conference speaker and is the co-author of the best-selling book *The Five Minute Failure*, various published articles and of the forthcoming book entitled *Coach the Executive Coach*.

Kevin's keen interest in sports led him into coaching athletes where success at the top level is as much in the mind as the skills. He has coached international sports people from a wide range of sports including Olympic, world and European record holders. He has also previously been the official PGA EURO PRO Golf Tour performance coach.

John Van Maurik

John van Maurik works on a wide range of management development and coaching initiatives focusing on leadership, strategy, change management, team building, communication skills and personal development.

As a coach he has been active since 1995 and has coached executives in both the private and public sectors. The range of people John has coached is very wide. While with PA Sundridge Park he was a director of the Leadership Programmes and as such established on-going coaching relationships with senior people from diverse businesses and has facilitated a number of strategy formulation workshops at board level.

As a writer, books published are *Discovering the Leader in You* (McGraw Hill. 1994), *The Portable Leader – how genuine leadership and teamwork can produce outstanding results*. (McGraw Hill. 1997), *The Effective Strategist* (Gower. 1999) and *Writers on Leadership* (Penguin 2001). As both a conference speaker and author, John has published many articles in journals and the national press as well as having broadcast on BBC radio.

As a trainer, John has worked extensively in both the private and public sectors and has travelled widely. He has run programmes in some 20 countries including the USA, South East Asia and the Indian sub-continent. John also spent 3 months on assignment to The Center for Creative Leadership, North Carolina.

contents

preface

It was a grey wet Friday afternoon and raindrops spattered against Misha's office window. The bleak weather matched her mood well as she sat staring out at the darkening sky – with *that* letter in her hand.

She choked back a sob.

"Don't be a fool!" she told herself. "You're nearly thirty and you are supposed to be on the fast track. What will other people think if you let them see you cry?"

And then there was an additional problem; Misha was a penguin – and penguins were notoriously thick-skinned and not supposed to know how to cry. But then in the animal world every species was getting in touch with their emotions these days. Many said it was too many trips to the human enclosure at the zoo that was doing it.

The office door was flung open and Mike, another penguin stormed in.

"Typical Mike," thought Misha. "Never bothers to knock."

Then she saw his face. His expression was an almost comic mixture of disappointment, confusion and anger. It would have been comic but for the fact that his eyes now glistened with what looked suspiciously like tears. But Mike cry? Not Mike, the brash, super confident go-getter. No way!

"I didn't get it!" he wailed.

Misha noticed that he had a letter under his wing. He waved it at her. "Would you believe it? I didn't get it!"

"Nether did I," replied Misha. "But I'm really surprised that you didn't. You were so confident. Not like me – they say here that it was my presentation that let me down."

"That's the reason they gave me as well," he replied. "I just don't get it. I don't have any trouble with presentations – in fact I find them dead easy."

Mike and Misha had spent the previous two days undergoing an assessment centre for promotion to management at Antarctic Foods, one of the premier organisations in the animal world. Both had been at the organisation for several years and whilst being highly competent at their jobs, promotion had so far eluded them. This was a disaster for them as Antarctic Foods usually employed and promoted penguins because of their specialist knowledge of fishing and cold storage.

For Mike especially this had been a frustrating experience and being a few years older than Misha, he had begun to wonder whether he had missed his opportunity. So, when Antarctic foods announced that promotion to management would now depend on candidates undergoing a formal assessment centre run by outside consultants, both had immediately volunteered.

The assessment centre, which had been run by a lion from Leonidas, the well-known firm of recruitment consultants and assessors, had consisted of a challenging variety of activities. They had built rafts to cross a stream, role played meetings with imaginary clients and been interviewed by a panel of expert assessors. Then as the finale, they had been asked to give a presentation during which they had to both talk on a subject of their own choice as well as put forward the case for their own promotion.

The presentation was the part that Misha had been dreading, but Mike had thought he would do particularly well at it.

"As I said," he grunted, "I just don't get it and now my career's going down the drain."

They both stared out at the rain. A large beast started to stalk across the car park. It was the chairman of the assessment panel, the Lion. He was a striking individual; he was purposeful and firm and he seemed to control any situation with an air of calm confidence.

"Just look at him," said Mike bitterly. "Typical Lion – he's finished, had his fun for the day and hasn't a clue about the chaos he's left behind him. He should be made accountable!"

"Well let's make him accountable," said Misha. "Let's ask him *why* we didn't make it. If our presentations let us down, what was it about them?"

They left Misha's office in a hurry and waddled splashing through the rain. It was something of a mad dash as the traffic was particularly bad for some reason. They were just in time to stop the lion from leaving.

He seemed amused. "You look like a couple of very flustered penguins. Now, how can I help you?"

This annoyed Misha even more. "We're not flustered," she replied. "But we are two very disappointed and confused birds who don't know what we did wrong."

"And it's all very well for you to leave, but what are we to do now?" added Mike.

The Lion smiled. "I can understand why you are frustrated. It was the presentation that let you both down, wasn't it?"

They nodded.

"As I thought Misha, I recall that you were like a timid mouse while you, Mike were so loud and brash that you reminded me of a donkey – or perhaps a bull in a china shop or even one of those penguin species from Africa, the Jackass."

"There's no need to be so personal," said Misha hotly. "I don't like being called a mouse!"

"I bet you are thinking: 'Typical consultant, driving off leaving us to pick up the pieces'. Well I'm not going to. Look, I'll meet you in the Safari Café across the road in ten minutes and I'll give you both more feedback and also some concrete advice. It's all for free, but there's one condition."

"What's that?" said Mike suspiciously.

"You listen to me and you act on my advice!" said the Lion.

Ten minutes later they met, and with Mike and Misha still looking very dubious, the Lion began to speak.

"We will meet a number of other animals in our discussions," the Lion said. "Some of them will be in your audience and some will be playing other roles."

"In that case you can be a seagull," said Mike. "Seagulls fly in, squawk a lot, drop guano and then fly out leaving a mess."

"Seagulls, eh? Well let me tell you Mike; only one of us is at sea here, and it's not me so pay attention," the Lion retorted with a curl of his lip that revealed the huge teeth underneath.

Mike resolved to do as he was told.

1

When to present – and what is a presentation anyway?

The Lion stared hard at the two penguins. They tried to stare back but his gaze was too severe, those tawny eyes too penetrating.

It felt as if they were at the animal academy for presenting and delivering and Misha wondered whether this was going to be like being back at school again.

On reflection, for her, school had been a challenge. The only chick of poor penguins, she had always felt compelled to succeed – even though she often doubted her ability to do so. This had spilled over into her career where she had tended to work harder than her male colleagues, sometimes being regarded as pushy and sometimes as insecure. Natural talent had got her as far as she had, but now her career had faltered.

Mike looked across at Misha, often they had been rivals but he wished he had got to know her better, but she seemed so remote and so hard to read. He had had more advantages than Misha, his parents were aristocratic Emperors coming from a larger iceberg, and he had travelled extensively on the ice flows as a fledgling and had gone to better schools. He had enjoyed sports and had hung around with some of the noisier polar bear cubs and more disreputable seals before starting his career.

Now finally he realised that advancement required concentration, dedication and effort. But what was the first thing to occur when he genuinely tried to get his act together? He had failed.

"So you want to learn how to present?" rumbled the Lion.

Presentations are inescapable

They nodded.

"Why?"

"Well," said Misha, "I just don't seem to be able to get away from them. I don't like doing them but in my business life they seem to be inescapable."

"That's right," added Mike. "I didn't think they worried me, but they do seem to feature quite heavily. I've had to give presentations to clients, customers, colleagues, bosses and even subordinates at a staff conference – that was like presenting to two hundred human nuns. Hey, I even had to give a presentation at my friend's wedding when I was his best penguin. You know, I really got through to the audience with some of my jokes, I . . ."

What is a presentation?

The Lion interrupted him.

"As you say, presentations, or public speaking can occur in many different situations. But how would you define a presentation – what is it?"

Mike and Misha both looked confused.

"Well like I said, it's about speaking in public," replied Misha. Then she added lamely: "Telling the audience things".

"I see that we shall have to start right at the beginning," the Lion said.

He paused for effect.

"A presentation is not just speaking in public. Unless you are a comedian who merely wants to make people laugh, *it is an act of persuasion*."

"Persuasion?" echoed Misha.

"Yes, persuasion! Whenever you first prepare to present you must first ask yourself the following question: '*What do I want the audience to say 'yes' to? What must they agree to at the end?*'".

"But why should they want to say yes?" interrupted Mike.

"Look, you impetuous penguin," growled the Lion, "when ever you set out to communicate – whatever the medium – you must have an objective. Even if you merely want those listening to be better informed about something you need to ask yourself: '*what will they need to know – what information must they have by the end*'. In your best penguin's speech you no doubt wanted to entertain the guests but you also no doubt wanted them to think that the groom was a splendid fellow and that he had chosen a wonderful penguin who was perfect in every way."

"I suppose I did, now that you put it that way."

"So when you set out to give a presentation in other circumstances such as in your business lives, it is even more important to have clear objectives. For example, give me some typical occasions when you may have to give a presentation."

"Well, there are sales presentations – getting prospective clients to buy our services," said Misha.

"And then there was the presentation that the animal resources koalas gave to managers to explain the new assessment centres," added Mike. "As well as the 'why we should be promoted' presentations we gave as part of the assessment centre itself."

"A few weeks ago I went to a conference," said Misha. "The koalas gave presentations on EU legislation and how it would affect our selling strategies. Then someone from a rival company to ours gave a presentation on how they had already used the legislation to gain a foothold in German markets."

The objectives – the act of persuasion

"Then don't you see that there are certain elements under-pinning all these different presentations?" the Lion asked. "For example, the wedding presentation sets out to entertain but also to convince penguins that the bride and groom have chosen wisely. The sales presentation obviously aims to persuade the undecided to buy your services or products. Finally the Koalas, in explaining the assessment centre approach, certainly wanted penguins like you to decide that it was a good way of evaluating your talents. Bringing it closer to home, your presentations at the centre must have had the objective of making others want to promote you."

"But what about the presentation on EU legislation?" countered Misha.

"It's still an act of persuasion," insisted the Lion. "Those presenting wanted you to adopt new approaches so as to be better exporters while the company that explained how they had already exploited the legislation wanted others to think that they had been forward thinking and fast moving – someone worthy of doing business with."

"But what about training – such as on training courses – that doesn't fit the bill!" said Mike triumphantly.

"If you don't realise that the trainer wants you to adopt new attitudes and behaviours, then there is no hope for you!" retorted the Lion.

He let out a snort of laughter. Mike's feathers were quite literally ruffled and he began to peck at them sullenly.

The Lion leaned forward on his haunches. "Presentations can take on many shapes and sizes, they can be given for a variety of reasons, but essentially they have one thing in common. . .

They are an act of Persuasion!

And the essential question you must ask as you start to prepare is...

'What do I want the audience to say 'yes' to?'"

The Lion gave the two penguins a piercing look from under his fierce brows.

"Do you agree? Do you say *'yes'* to what I have said?"

Meekly they both nodded.

"Good, now that we have agreed on the definition and purpose – the *'whats'* and the *'whys'* – lets move on to discuss the *'hows'*."

2

Nerves – confronting the butterflies of fear

"So now that we have defined what a presentation is," said the Lion, "let's move on to talk about how to do it."

"Hold on!" exclaimed Misha. "You're going far too fast. There's something vital we need to deal with first and there's no point in going ahead until we do so."

"And that is?" said the Lion.

"Why nerves, of course!"

Mike butted in. "Typical. You would jump at your own shadow. Sometimes you've just got to go ahead and do it."

"No. Misha has got a point," said the Lion. "Most penguins do suffer from nerves before giving a presentation. It's only natural to have a few butterflies in your stomach."

"Butterflies!" groaned Misha. "I get on well with butterflies – they did a great job decorating my house. This is more like one of those road races the cheetahs seem to like so much."

The effect of nerves

"What effect does it have?" the Lion asked.

"Well, I get a cold feeling in the pit of my stomach, my pulse races, my mouth goes dry and I sometimes even forget what it was I was going to say. And that's only for a start!"

Mike looked puzzled but the Lion appeared to smile.

"I understand. In fact standing up and speaking in public has generally been accepted as one of life's most feared events.

In the USA presentations are the number 1 public phobia and in the UK they are number 2. In fact spiders are number 1 in the UK, perhaps we should get you to do a presentation to spiders."

The Lion's smile broadened.

"So, many fear presentations far more than having a car smash, an operation or giving birth – some fear it more than death itself."

"How pathetic," said Mike. "I don't get nerves, I just go for it."

"And that may well be part of your problem," said the Lion. "A certain level of nerves, or adrenalin, is useful; it stimulates better performance. For example, the human, Dave Grossman, found that the optimum state of arousal was a heart rate of between 115 and 145 beats per minute. If you are towards the top of the adrenalin level then the endorphins created will increase your speed and strength and even act as a pain killer.

"It's when the heart rate exceeds 175 that it takes on a negative effect and the individual gets shaky and feels exhausted. So it's only when the butterflies get out of hand that they become destructive."

Self-fulfilling prophecies

"My problem," said Misha, "is that I get really worried about failure, then the worry makes me hesitate, stammer, then lose my place and the only way I can get through it is by speaking faster and faster and faster and…"

"And it becomes a self-fulfilling prophecy," concluded the Lion.

"Exactly."

Mike was intrigued.

"Do you mean to say that before they present, some penguins pace up and down saying to themselves: '*I can't present,*

I'm no good at it, I always mess it up!' and so when they do in fact mess it up they say *'There! I told you so. I'm no good so I must avoid all future opportunities to present'?"*

"Exactly," replied the Lion. "It's called an Implicative Dilemma."

"You sound like the owls with that kind of jargon," said Mike.

Mike didn't like the owls; they were so damn clever they made him feel decidedly inferior.

"Maybe I do, but it's a useful concept," said the Lion. "You convince yourself that you are unable to do something that worries you. You give it a try (carrying all the negatives that you have just loaded onto yourself) and then when you don't do too well you somehow congratulate yourself for living up to your negative expectations – and use that as an excuse for never trying again."

"Now that's quite interesting," said Mike. "I can buy that concept."

"Yes. But how do you break the hold of this implicative dilemma?" said Misha.

"Well for a start you must remember that the audience is almost always on your side," the Lion said. "They want you to succeed because your success will give them the information they need in a relaxed and enjoyable way. If you are obviously struggling this will only embarrass them – and they don't want that for themselves, or for you!"

"So some nerves, or butterflies, are OK!" said Mike. "But not when they take over. Right?"

Butterflies flying in formation

"Right," said the Lion. "I recall the case of Group Captain Douglas Bader, the human World War Two flying Ace. After the war, as a legless hero, he spent a lot of time speaking in public in order to raise money for the disabled.

He spoke well, and on one occasion someone rather enviously asked him whether *he* ever got butterflies in his stomach. '*Of course I do,*' replied the old ace. '*But I quickly teach them to fly in formation*'."

Mike and Misha laughed.

"Now," said the Lion. "Let's teach *your* butterflies to fly in formation. The difference between nerves and excitement is the direction that your butterflies fly."

The Lion let out a loud "Roarrrrrrrrr!!"

The penguins jumped about three feet in the air, nearly leaving their feathers behind. They immediately felt their butterflies fly forward in a round circular motion. They felt negative, nervous and exhausted.

"Now concentrate on the butterflies and imagine making them fly in a backwards, circular motion," the Lion said.

They concentrated hard and suddenly they both felt positive, calmer and energised. Even Mike had to admit it was amazing.

"What happens if my butterflies are flying in another direction or not circling at all?"

"Look, it's easy really," said the Lion, who was beginning to

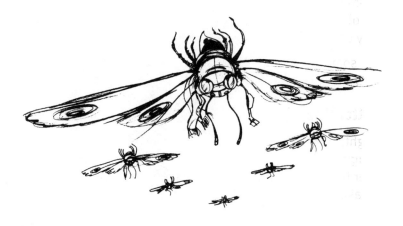

feel he was getting through to these birds. "You can use these thoughts about flying and formation to both calm you and organise you further. Think about those butterflies in more detail. What colour are they? What would happen if you were to paint them a different colour? What do they look like in flight if they were to fly in a different formation? A formation that works even better for you! Before you know where you are, you are using your initial nerves to help you control and organise the whole presentation. Oh the power of positive visualisation!"

3

Beating your nerves – mental preparation and herding the animals

"As I said many of us get nerves," continued the Lion. "But that's no excuse and it's up to us to deal with them."

"But what if the butterflies refused to fly in formation?" asked Misha, who was still anxious.

"Well for a start," replied the Lion, "you could *rationalise* them."

The penguins stared back at him blankly.

"Well, consider flying. Penguins have an irrational fear of flying. In fact, they are not afraid of flying – they are afraid of crashing. Similarly, they might say they are afraid of snakes, when in reality they are afraid of being bitten."

Mike came close to pointing out that penguins couldn't fly for love nor money, but thought better of pointing this out, since he could see what the Lion was getting at. He settled for saying: "But so what?"

"Well the solution to the fear lies in the second part of the statement," the Lion replied. "In reality, flying is the safest form of transport. The servicing and maintenance of aircraft is always done to the highest standard and the pilots are trained to the nth degree. You are in far more danger of being knocked down when you cross the road to post a letter than of being involved in a plane crash.

"And why do penguins that handle snakes rarely get bitten? The reason is that they have received special training and advice. They know what to do, what equipment to use and what precautions to take. In short, our initial perception of risk is often totally unrealistic and acts as a barrier."

"But how does that relate to my fear of presentations?" asked Misha.

"Quite simply it is the fact that all of these penguins, whether they be pilots or snake handlers, have one thing in common and that is *control*. They are in control of both the activity and of their mental state. They know what they are doing, where they are going, have planned how they will get there and are managing their resources. It is like going on holiday; you always pack first."

"I'm beginning to see," said Misha. "Overcoming your fear of making presentations is much the same. It must involve planning what you have to do and then taking control of both your resources and your mental state."

"At last – we have breakthrough!" roared the Lion with delight.

"No, not quite yet," said Misha. "I can see the need for taking control, but how to do so beats me."

The steps to mental preparation

The Lion became serious. "I also coach the athletes at the animal Olympics and a number of professional sports teams," he said. "The same thing that would hold back a penguin competing at their peak in the water polo or scoring a perfect ten in the diving is the same thing that would hold you back from presenting. There are a number of steps to good mental preparation and while some of them may appear rather bizarre, I can assure you they work."

self talk

"The first step is called **self talk**. Here it is important to catch you talking to yourself in a negative way. You could try changing all your negative statements into positive statements about what is to come. For example, instead of saying 'I'm dreading the presentation I'm faced with today, it's bound to go wrong', say: 'I'm really excited about the presentation, it's going to be great'. Now for some, that is all that is necessary. But if you have a bad dose of anxiety that does not respond to a positive statement, you could try debunking your anxiety."

"It's like this," said the Lion. "Catch yourself making negative statements and then repeat them to yourself in a ridiculously high-pitched voice, like a duck, then a squeaky mouse and then an absurdly exaggerated foreign accent. Soon you will find yourself laughing at the anxiety. That is the time to give yourself a positive stroke and say: 'Relax. Keep Calm'. You will find that you respond to your own advice and are still laughing at your anxiety when the time comes to present."

the spot

"As we know the mind and body are one," the Lion said. "Next is a more physical technique, if this one is OK for Olympic athletes then it is OK for you. It's called *the spot* or *peripheral vision*.

"Often when you are very nervous, you over-heat, your heart races and feels like it is pounding in your head and coming out of your chest. To calm it down fix your stare at a single spot, and whilst staring at that spot become aware of what is happening at either side of you in your peripheral vision. Then you will find that as your pulse slows you gain a more relaxed perspective about what you are about to do, and your heart stops – thankfully not completely, but the heavy pounding disappears. In other words, you calm down."

"How does that work?" asked Misha.

"It comes from the fight and flight response, when our ancestors were first hunting or being hunted," replied the Lion. "When hunting, they needed narrow or 'foveal vision' as it is known, to fix on the animal to enable them to get their prey. Similarly when running away they needed to fix on a landmark in the distance to ensure that they took the straightest and fastest route to get away. When they were relaxed and resting their vision needed to be wide, enabling them to see what was happening around them. So when you stare at the spot and widen your vision it allows you to feel relaxed.

The DBC

"Now let me tell you about the third technique – *the DBC*. You have heard the term 'being centred', I imagine. The most vulnerable part of our body is the stomach; this is the same with all animals.

"Think of prey, where do predators attack them? In the stomach because the rest of the body has bone to protect it."

For once Mike was quite willing to accept that the 400lbs of muscle sitting in front of him knew exactly what he was talking about. He involuntarily wrapped himself tightly in his flippers.

"This also stems from the old fight or flight syndrome which happens to us naturally."

"Hold on what is the fight of flight syndrome and why do we feel this way?" asked Misha.

The Lion turned slowly to his penguin charges and bared his teeth, just to set the mood.

"There's a very good reason for all the changes that come over you when you are under stress," he said. "I'm going to write this out for you because it's very interesting and makes for good pub conversation."

The Lion took a napkin and began to write with a pen he had cleverly hidden in his mane. Mike wondered two things: how could the Lion write so well with those giant paws and what

else this mighty beast had hidden in that mass of well-coiffed hair.

Unaware of these profound considerations the Lion wrote a list to show just what happens when anxiety or panic takes over and the 'fight or runaway (flight)' reaction kicks in:

The heart starts to beat faster. This is to pump blood faster to where the body needs it, such as thighs and biceps but away for the bodies extremities such as the fingers. This is to make you less likely to bleed to death if injured and explains the cold, clammy hands experienced by feeling anxious.

Breathing speeds up to get more oxygen to the muscles. This can lead to a choking sensation or feeling light-headed. The body sweats so it will not over-heat if an attack actually happens.

Also, being slippery means it's far harder for a predator to grab hold of you. The brain releases a chemical called cortisol which shuts down the part of the brain responsible for creativity so you can focus completely on the moment and your immediate surroundings.

"Like anything, it's much easier to find a solution if you know what's behind it," the Lion said.

The penguins were indeed impressed; even Mike had stopped trying to peer into the Lion's mane to try and find evidence of a kitchen sink and was nodding intently.

The result of these symptoms is that your centre rises and you get the dry throat and for some the butterflies start. The answer is to *re-centre* yourself and break the build up of tension.

"The technique is simple; you tense or squeeze your back-side muscles, relax them, and then relax again. All at once you will feel your centre drop and then again and you will feel centred and calmer. Now do it again and as you relax your backside and relax again put your hand onto your stomach and feel your centre drop. There you have it: The Double Bum Clench."

visualising

"The next method of mental preparation is that of *visualising* what success will look and feel like. This is a technique which has been used by golfers and athletes to visualise the perfect future event; to think what it will be like as you achieve success.

"You need to think of all the things that you would you feel, hear, see and notice when you hit the perfect golf shot or score the winning goal or give that confident presentation. In doing so, you create the model behaviour for your future performance and then all you have to do is to act out the behaviour to achieve the model.

"All you then do is to practise, visualising time and time

again running the movie in your mind. You are programming yourself to act in that way when the event actually happens.

"Researchers have undertaken studies on athletes who have practised this method of mental preparation. Electrodes were placed on their bodies and the same micro muscles moved as when they were actually doing the activity, event or competition. You see the mind does not know the difference between reality and what is a visualisation. That is why we feel so scared when we watch horror movies.

"In fact, one of those humans was fighting in the Vietnam War and was captured. To keep himself sane, he played golf in his mind each day. One day he would play well, the next not so, he would get out of bunkers and hit marvellous tee-shots and putts. After three years he was released."

For a second the Lion mulled over how humans always seemed to be attacking each other. He was pleased common sense had prevailed and they had been confined to zoos.

"Don't tell me, the first thing he did when he got back was to play golf," said Mike.

"No, he had a wash, saw his family and was debriefed," roared the Lion in delight at his poor joke.

Fortunately no one pointed out how poor this humour was as it was well-known in the animal world that it was a bad idea to tell a lion his jokes weren't funny. It just wasn't the done thing if you wanted to remain in one piece.

The Lion pressed on after his mirth had subsided: "Then he played golf. He hit the best round of his life by 4 shots, yet he had not played for 3 years."

"Yes, I like all of that," said Misha, "but it still doesn't deal with the fact that the audience may be difficult and make all this mental preparation irrelevant."

"It will never be irrelevant," said the Lion. "But you are right, we do need to look at the composition of the audience. Maybe it would help if we thought of the types of animals you might be faced with."

"As far as I'm concerned," said Misha with a shudder, "there is only one sort of animal in the audience and that is a leopard seal and it's waiting for me to fall off the ice flow as soon as the presentation begins."

"Nonsense," said Mike, and for once the Lion agreed with him.

"Audiences come in many shapes and sizes – let's look at the types of animal they might contain, and more importantly, how to deal with them."

Dealing with a difficult audience – the animals

"First of all there is the *Bulldog*. These are the aggressive types who always want to win. Often they have not understood the point and the best way to win them over is to use other members of the group to reinforce the point you are trying to make.

"You do this by creating discussion, asking questions and gaining different perspectives, explanations and insights into your subject.

"However, if the bulldog is persistent or really appears to be looking for a fight it would be better not to draw on the audience but to wait until a break and have a confidential conversation with them. Find out what their reasoning is and what concerns they have. By giving them feedback and explaining the impact of their behaviour on the rest of the group it can make them aware of the damage they are doing.

"Bulldogs are often not the most self-aware of animals and do not realise the impact they have on others. At all times keep cool. If they say something constructive and you give them positive feedback it will make it far harder for them to be difficult.

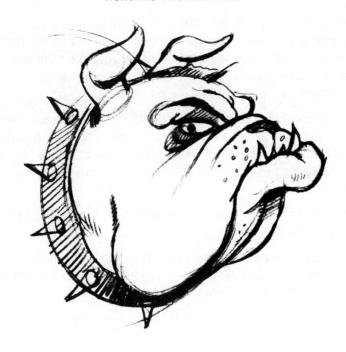

"So look for the positive; try to find out what the intention behind that animal's behaviour might be. For example, ask yourself the following questions: 'Exactly what is it this individual is objecting to?' You need to be clear about this. Then ask yourself: 'What might this individual be trying to resolve? What do they need?'

"The answers to these questions might help you get to the fundamental issue which is: '*What is the purpose behind the difficult behaviour*?' Answer that one and you will be well on the way to defusing the situation. And isn't that more respectful and honourable than ignoring these individuals or seeking to put them down?"

Since penguins aren't really equipped for a scrap with any-one, let alone a bulldog, both Misha and Mike rather warmed to this advice.

"Next there is the *Horse*. Horses are keen and enthusiastic as well as intelligent but the risk is that they might interrupt too much. Taking up one of their statements and turning it into a group discussion is one way of encouraging them whilst also keeping the session on track.

"However, if they come too much into the fore others in the audience may become irritated so you need to make it quite clear that everyone will have an opportunity to say something. Doing this is far more likely to get you their general buy in."

"So like any good car, you have to harness the horse power," giggled Mike.

Unfortunately penguins are not in the position to make bad jokes and get away with it that lions are and Mike's joke led to an embarrassing silence.

"Yes, quite," said the Lion with an air of superiority borne of being top of the foodchain.

"But horses can become *Artful Monkeys* – or know-it-alls. If you have one of them, use them. Present though them, let them do some of the talking, but be careful because at some stage you may need to intervene as the monkeys who love playing to an audience may take over or disrupt by wishing to appear funny, wise and/or knowledgeable. They may attempt to show they are better than their colleagues and even you – if you give counter examples, remain respectful! You might wish to say something like 'yes that is right for your organisation, or part of the organisation', and acknowledge what they are saying, then give examples of other organisations – try to make them understand that in general their view point may not apply. But be careful because you don't want to offend them."

"But not everybody is going to be a pest, surely!" said Misha with more hope than conviction.

"Of course not," replied the Lion. "But you don't need help

35

with the helpful ones, do you? Take the *Gazelle*, for instance. They are actually too timid and retiring to be helpful. You could leave them alone and they will do no harm. On the other hand, it is even better if you make them feel important in the eyes of the group, say, by asking their opinions or asking questions which you know they will be able to answer, then their confidence will grow and they often give insights and perspectives others will not have seen. By making your presentation interactive this will also raise the energy in the audience. Remember asking questions can often be the answer. They will thank you for it and be a future ally."

"Against whom?" said Mike. "Are there any other vicious predators out there?"

"Oh yes, a few. Take the *Hedgehog* for example. They can cause you more harm than you might think. They are prickly, often sceptical and tend to make no attempt to hide the fact

that they are not interested. Also to start with they are seldom interested in anyone else's ideas. You have to listen to them first and listen to their objections as some might be relevant.

"Once they feel understood their minds will start to open – remember minds are like parachutes and only open. Perhaps try to get them talking about something to do with their work. Give them an opportunity to get their ideas accepted and this will in turn enable them to listen to the opinions of others.

"The *Mice* can also be fun, they often sit at the back or the side quietly whispering. Sometimes they talk about the subject in hand, but other times they talk about shopping or their social life at the same time as you are presenting or facilitating a group discussion.

"This can easily be avoided by agreeing the format at the start of the presentation including when you will or will not take questions etc. You may wish to suggest that at any one time there will only be one conversation going on in the room and it will involve you. Alternatively at the time of the whispering you could involve them in the wider group discussion by asking them if they would like to share their thoughts with the group.

"Finally there is the *Fox*. Foxes are crafty and enjoy setting traps or slipping a banana skin in your path. In general it is best not to tackle them head on, as they will always find a way of escaping. Try saying something like: '*Oh yes, and what do other audience members think*?' You will find that others have recognised the Fox and will usually side with you."

"You make it sound like a minefield," said Mike.

But this time Misha interrupted him before he had time for a good whinge.

"A minefield perhaps, but at least we've been shown a way across it," she said.

Understanding difference

"Yes and remember, 99% of the time these animals only show their positive traits, it is rare for the negatives to surface," the Lion said. "In fact, the real value of this information is allowing you to understand where others are coming from. To realise audience members are not so much difficult, but different. If we understand these differences we can also learn the positive intention behind the behaviours.

"I'll give you one extra tip. It's back to mental preparation. This one works especially well in the middle of presentations when you are perhaps faced with a Fox or Hedgehog. Think of a *positive event* in your life, maybe sometime when you were feeling really positive, had a sense of achievement, felt relaxed or were with people you totally trusted – basically anytime something went especially well for you. Recapture the good feelings, the happiness and the positive thoughts you felt about yourself and your ability to achieve at that time.

"Imagine you are there right now, seeing what you saw,

hearing what you heard and feeling what you felt inside. You will then feel that way again. It will have to be a very prickly Hedgehog that can penetrate that wall of positivity. The good feelings will carry you through the storm – in fact they should last until the presentation is over. You can also use this as part of your pre-presentation preparation."

At that stage the bartender, a rather attractive blonde Afghan hound, rather pointedly asked the trio whether they would like another drink. Mike brought a round of soft drinks as the Lion had to get back to the plains and the penguins both knew how embarrassing it would be if they were caught swimming over the limit on their way back to the icebergs.

4
Preparing your Presentation

They sipped their cordials and then Mike broke the silence.

"That's more helpful than I thought it would be," he said. "But somehow I don't think it's the whole story."

"Agreed," said Misha. "I can see how all that psychological stuff can help me get my mind straight, but it doesn't help me get my *presentation* straight."

"Oh ye of little faith," groaned the Lion in exasperation. "It's not *meant* to, you puerile penguins. But how are you going to get your presentation straight if your mind is all in a mess?"

All these interruptions made the Lion feel the penguins might be a better aperitif than he had previously thought. Then he remembered he was a professional and eating the clients' staff would definitely be frowned upon.

With a deep breath he continued in a more moderate tone.

The plan

"Look, once you no longer feel flustered you can do some realistic planning. You can truly organise your thoughts. Shall we give it a try?"

Mike and Misha nodded.

"OK, imagine that you are about to start planning a presentation. What is the first thing that you must do?"

"Find out whether I'm going to get paid for doing it?" suggested Mike.

"Or whether I can get out of doing it?" added Misha.

"No, you bird brains," roared the Lion. "You must decide on

the subject matter – the title. In other words, the key things that you want the audience to say 'yes' to. The governing thought if you like. Once you have decided on that, all the other elements start to fall into place. First and last impressions count, ensure you know the first sentence and the very last sentence of your presentation, word for word and off by heart."

Mike and Misha looked blank so the Lion took a piece of paper out of his briefcase and began to draw on it something that looked remarkably like a family tree. The Lion put the sketch in front of the penguins.

"Remember, it is the 80/20 rule – 80% preparation and only 20% actual presentation. Look at this diagram. The governing thought is like the CEO and it dictates the rest of the content. Under the CEO come the directors and they are the main subject areas you wish to cover. Under the directors will come the staff and the staff members will form the content of the presentation."

The Lion scribbled on and the family tree began to grow.

"So you line the content up under the main subject areas and then lo and behold, the presentation starts to take shape."

"That's brilliant!" said Mike. "I can see my presentation really starting to take shape."

Misha began to draw her own family tree and then stopped.

"I've tried to plan a fairly basic presentation about my department and suddenly I'm snowed under with information. How on earth will I fit it all in?"

"Maybe you won't have to," continued the Lion. "One thing most penguins worry about is ending too soon and so they pack their presentations with facts and content. In reality, most presenters overrun. Time plays funny tricks on you when you are presenting and so the key thing is to put all the facts and features down under the most applicable subject areas and then start sorting them and deleting."

"Sorting? Deleting?" Mike looked puzzled.

"Absolutely! Once you have got all the possible facts and contents down you can then sort them into:

Prioritising

- The **Musts** – those things that are essential, the presentation will be incomplete without them

- The **Oughts** – things that give colour and body to the presentation

- The **Nice to Haves** (but not really necessary) – those things worth including but only if time permits. These are things like anecdotes or additional examples."

The Lion saw that he had their attention. "Why not give it a try?" he said.

Both Mike and Misha spent some time working on their hypothetical plans, crouched low over their notepads, beaks clamped shut in concentration.

"If it helps," said the Lion, "keep in mind the following key question: *what is the one thing that I want the audience to go away remembering*?"

"Hey, this planning is demanding," complained Mike eventually. "I just want to get on and do it."

"There are certain benefits to allotting time to planning," said the Lion with exaggerated patience. "The benefits to properly planning your presentation are that you will look calm and in control during it. In addition, you will run to the allotted time, the material will flow and be easy to follow and the points you cover will be relevant to the audience.

"Finally, you will be seen as a credible subject expert. This is called 'benefit language' and is a really good way for a presenter to think. It works for both the presenter and the audience."

Mike's feathers turned a shade of red.

"Now that you put it like that, I suppose I must agree," he conceded.

Misha spoke up: "This is useful, I'm beginning to feel more confident about what to put in and I'm even beginning to see where I may be able to 'wow' the audience. But how on earth will I be able to remember it all?"

She held up a large scrappy piece of paper. "Do I take this in with me?"

The Lion shook his tawny head, his mane rippling majestically.

"Certainly not! It would be recipe for disaster. Apart from the fact that you would not be able to follow it, it would act as an amplifier for your nerves – even the slightest shake in your hand would be magnified by it and the audience would spot your nerves a mile away."

He held up the paper and it wavered, even in the Lion's rock steady paw.

"Hmmm – I see," said Mike. "Or rather I can't see your paw shaking, but I can see the paper shaking. But what do we do then?"

"This is where CUE CARDS come into play," replied the Lion.

"So you write it all down onto little cards and read it off them?" asked Misha.

"Yes and no," replied the Lion and held out some small rectangular cards for them to look at.

"The top part is where you write your opening sentence, word for word. This is just in case you should get totally tongue tied at the very start and forget what to say completely."

"That's useful for me," commented Misha. "I've always been scared of that happening."

"Well, you should always know the first sentence of your presentation off by heart and your last. This will make a great first and lasting impression. Having got over that hurdle, the rest is organisation," said the Lion.

"On the left hand side you put your running notes, such as when to change to another visual aid, when to put in stories or anecdotes you might wish to add."

He jotted down some more notes.

"Look, I've summarised everything we have covered so far about planning, just as if I was preparing to do a presentation on it."

"I like it! I like it!" enthused Mike. "But what is that note there about clarity and understanding – and what's that about Fog Factors on the right hand side?"

"I'm jumping ahead of myself," said the Lion. "Listen: a basic principle of all communication is that it is not *communicated* until it is *understood*. So before you plan, try to assess just how much the audience are likely to know about the subject. For example, are they experts? Or pretty ignorant? If they are ignorant and you fill your presentation with jargon and technicalities you will just baffle them and bore them. So the right hand side is for additional reminders and special notes for yourself."

"Understood," said Misha. "But you still haven't explained the Fog Factor."

Good communication – avoiding the fog factor

"Many presenters have a tendency to use longer words than are necessary, to show off by using language that they would not use on a day-to-day basis," the Lion replied. "Then they are surprised when they are not understood. Small wonder!"

"I can recall a quote by that human playwright, George Bernard Shaw," said Mike somewhat grandiosely. "It goes something like: *'The problem with most communication is the assumption that it has been successfully achieved'*."

"Ah, words of wisdom at last!" laughed the Lion. "And of course the antidote to the Fog Factor is KISS. This stands for Keep it Short and Simple or even Keep it Simple, Stupid! And if I can get you to accept that, then we can move onto the next stage."

"Consider it ACE'd," replied Mike.

For once the Lion looked confused.

"ACE'd?" He asked.

"Accepted, convincing and energising!" replied Mike. "Words that should apply to all presentations, don't you think? How do you stop people falling asleep or the energy dropping really low in the room?"

"Great question," said the Lion. "When you use your peripheral vision, if you see someone shuffle or move, turn and present to them, then the next person who fidgets turn to them. It is a technique great presenters use. It makes the audience feel like the presenter is actually presenting to them. It also stops the lighthouse effect when the presenter continuously moves their head around the audience back from side to side."

5
Places and practising

"So that's it then," said Mike. "How to prepare. I must say I like the cards. So now we're ready to go for it."

"Do you think that's all the preparation that's necessary?" asked the Lion.

"There must be more to preparation than that," said Misha, who knew a rhetorical question when she heard one.

"So what might be missing?" quizzed the Lion.

The venue

"Well for a start, I'm always a bit nervous until I've seen where the presentation is going to take place," said Misha. "For example, it might be quite unsuitable and either too big or too small."

"And if it's the wrong size," chipped in Mike, "it might make using your visual aids difficult."

"Well there we have it," said the Lion. "Vital steps of the preparation include getting to know the venue and deciding what sort of visual aids to use. Let's talk about that.

"If you can, always check out the room, or venue before the presentation. Some venues are designed to make it easy for the presenter while others unfortunately are not. Useful things to look for are the positions of the windows and where bright light is likely to come from, whether the room is big enough to sit the number of people you expect, where the power supply will come from, whether there is a podium or rostrum (and whether you actually want one) and whether there is enough space for you to operate from."

"I suppose an important aspect is whether you can achieve the right distance from the audience," said Misha.

"What do you mean by that?" asked Mike.

"Well you don't want them to be sitting on your lap, but on the other hand you don't want to be too distant from them," Misha replied.

"Agreed," said the Lion. "And what is more the size and quality of the room may influence the type of visual aids you are able to use."

"Now that's the bit I like," said Mike. "I really enjoy wowing people with my hi-tech visual presentations. I can get words

and pictures arriving on the screen from all angles – I can even build in sound effects as they do so."

"And by doing that you may well be falling into the old trap of putting the media before the message," interrupted the Lion. "Look, a visual aid is just what it says – it is an aid to, not the purpose of the presentation. You need to assess what the audience expects."

"What do you mean by that?" asked a confused Misha.

"Well, if they expect a short informal briefing they will probably think a real bells and whistles presentation to be overkill. On the other hand, if you are designing a sales presentation with the object of showing your firm up in a good light, then you should invest time in preparing a presentation that is enhanced by up-to-date technology. Yet again, if you wanted to design a highly interactive session where you sounded out other people's views then perhaps a flip chart is all you need. Flip charts lend an air of informality and always encourage group participation."

"So we have choices," said Mike.

"Exactly. Making a presentation work is like making a cake; you have to have the right ingredients in the right measures."

Practising – stagger, walk and run

"You keep mentioning the need to practise," said Misha.

"Indeed and once again a few simple tips will make all the difference," said the Lion. "You could divide your practising into stages. First of all is the *Stagger Through*.

"This is where you go through the presentation, finding out where all the difficult bits are, making mistakes, correcting them and generally by trial and error finding out what works. It is best if you can have a sympathetic friend to give you feedback and advice as you stagger through."

"Then there is the *Walk Through*. This is where you go through the whole presentation as well as you can, but still stop to put things right where needed and to receive feedback. Here you are still building the presentation, still putting on the finishing touches.

"The Walk Through will lead you on to the *Run Through*. This is to all intents and purposes the final rehearsal. At this stage do not stop and ask for feedback, do not re-arrange items but give the presentation as you would on the day itself. You can still get feedback from your friend afterwards but it is important to practice the whole thing both for your own peace of mind and also to get the actual timings sorted out.

"However, remember this: *do not over practise*. Never go through it at the run through stage more than three times. The brain then over-learns it and starts to work on autopilot, thus ironing out all opportunities for creativity and improvisation as you are going along. It will be like reading the alphabet backwards."

"So that's that then?" asked Mike.

Amplification or not

"Almost. At some stage you may need to work out whether you need amplification, or not. This will depend on both the quality of the venue as well as the size of the audience. You never know whether the venue transmits or kills sound and the only way to find out is to visit the venue beforehand, get your friend to stand at the back and then talk to him

or her. If you can be clearly heard you may not need any amplification."

"You said 'may'," said Mike.

"Exactly – in an acoustically good room you should not need amplification with up to 50 people present. Between 50 and 100 will probably need it and with over 100 you most certainly will need it."

"Supposing I just talk more loudly?" said Mike. "My voice carries well."

"I don't care whether you are Pavarottweiler, Jose Carerrasp, or even Placido Domingoat," said the Lion. "There is enough shuffling, coughing and muttering from 100 people to ensure that even the loudest voices don't reach the back. However, if you are relying solely on your voice, try dropping the volume as well – this can force people to listen! And now I think we *are* done with that particular subject."

At that stage the waitress loped over to their table. Clearly they were doing a lot of talking and not much spending.

"Do we have much more to cover?" Mike inquired.

"A fair amount," replied the Lion. "Perhaps we should get something to eat before we go on."

So Mike and Misha ordered fish while the Lion ordered venison steak, rare.

"I'll give you some more tips while we wait for our food," he said hungrily.

6

Giving the presentation

The waitress trotted off and they could hear her barking their orders out to the chef. Like in all good cafés the chef was an octopus who was putting all his arms to good use to assure quick service.

The Lion turned back to Mike and Misha.

"And now let's talk about the bit you've both been waiting for. Let's go over actually delivering the presentation."

Mike clapped his flippers together. "At last! I thought we'd never get round to it. All that stuff we've had to plough through about planning and equipment..."

"Yes, but if you didn't plan or didn't think about your visual aids *before* you actually stand up in front of the audience, you would probably end up in a terrible mess," the Lion said.

"Now, I want to divide the actual techniques of delivery into a number of separate but overlapping areas."

He started to tick them off with his claws. They included:

- breathing
- use of voice
- the power of language
- the non-verbal elements of communication and control
- and finally, handling questions

Mike and Misha nodded and the Lion squared his gigantic shoulders before starting while a group of gazelles on a nearby table eyed him suspiciously.

Breathing

"First of all, let's look at breathing. We can so often let ourselves down at this very basic level. For example, many presenters breathe from the top of their lungs. Thus the lungs do not open fully. This means the presenter runs out of air at exactly the wrong moment and has to breathe in again, sometimes sounding like a gasp.

"Breathing should be centred at the bottom of the lungs. Drawing breath into this area will make more air available and you will feel more in control and better able to control your tension.

"To create the right effect, focus on the idea of breathing from your belly, as if your mouth was there. Never force your breathing and never try to hold your breath. The more you breathe out the easier it is to breathe in again."

"That seems to go against everything I was taught to do when diving for fish," said Mike.

The Lion ignored him and continued.

The Voice

"O.K. let's look at the elements of voice. The voice and the content make up for about one third of the total impact in face-to-face communication. On the telephone, however, the voice contributes up to three quarters of the overall meaning – that is why telesales people are taught to smile as they make their pitch; it makes their voice sound more relaxed and friendly. There are however, supposed to be five distinct and controllable elements in our voices.

Pitch

The first is *pitch*. This is the musical quality of one's voice, the way it rises and falls across a sentence or phrase. There are a number of common variations in pitch and these are most noticeable at the end of a sentence. For example, *going up in pitch* implies a question and therefore injects a note of uncertainty – it elicits a response from the listener. But a lot of presenters do not vary the pitch at all. What effect do you think that has?"

"I guess it sounds boring and maybe implies a lack of interest or enthusiasm on the part of the presenter," volunteered Mike.

"Exactly!" said the Lion and illustrated it with a low continuous rumbling growl. At this the gazelles at the nearby table started to look increasingly panicked. One called for their bill even though their meal of vegetarian cannelloni was unfinished.

"But I want to know how to be more commanding," said Misha.

"That's easy," said the Lion. "Listen. Going down in pitch at the end of a phrase is commanding and implies inner confidence." He illustrated this with an assertive growl.

Volume

"And this of course brings us on to the whole issue of *volume*," the Lion said. "You may have experienced people who shout so loudly on the phone that you have to hold the receiver a foot away from your ear. On the other hand some people speak so softly that you have to keep asking them to repeat themselves. Neither is good – the ideal volume in a presentation is somewhere between medium and loud. Any louder than that and you will sound aggressive." (He looked hard at Mike at this point who attempted a nonchalant shrug). "Any softer and you will sound as if you lack confidence."

This time he stole a glance at Misha, who blushed and nodded.

Speed

"And then there is the speed of delivery," continued the Lion.

"The speed of voice is the rate of words per minute that you speak. Although certain dialects may encourage faster speech than others, as a general rule, if you speak too slowly you may sound rather simple and speak too fast and you may sound nervous or impatient.

"As a general rule, speak more slowly than your normal talking speed and pause at the end of each point. This gives the audience more time to think about what you have said. And think about your tone. Research has shown that 38 per cent of impact lies in the speaker's tone and only 7 per cent in the actual words used."

The Lion gave Mike and Misha a steely look. "Both of you in the past tended to fluff your delivery. Take it steady!"

"But I'm worried about sounding *boring*!" Misha squealed.

"There's no need to fear that," replied the Lion. "All you have to do is release the *energy* that you can easily put into your voice."

"Energy?" said Misha, who was still not convinced.

"Yes this is the amount of **oooooooooOOOMPH** in your voice. It gives that feeling of interest, sincerity and enthusiasm. This energy comes from your breathing. If you breathe from the top of your chest (shallow breathing) you will not have enough energy in your voice. Try using your stomach muscles when you breathe and notice the difference – energy will fall naturally into your conversation and at the start of a new sentence or change in subject, it will be easy to inject energy into your voice. Listen."

The Lion gave a series of energised growls and at this the gazelles' orderly retreat became a rout. Within seconds they had stampeded out of the café, not bothering to wait for their change in their haste.

The waitress arrived to bring them their food and, having picked up the considerable change from the gazelle's table gave the Lion a broad smile.

"I *do* hope you like your meat, sir," she said, "You can come back *anytime*!"

The Lion smiled benignly: "And that neatly brings us on to the subject of *articulation*," he concluded. "How do we know she was sincere?"

"Because she articulated the words 'do' and 'anytime' with more emphasis and more clearly than the others," said Mike.

"Quite. Articulation is the effect the muscles in your mouth have on your voice. On the telephone you can hear when someone is smiling, this is because different muscles are employed. On the other hand you may notice that when too much alcohol is consumed, the voice becomes slurred as the muscles have become too relaxed."

At this stage a bloodhound staggered across to the bar and demanded another pint of strong ale with a very slurred bark. The waitress refilled the dog's bowl and went about her business.

"See what I mean?" asked the Lion. "Articulation and control are most important. Actors, singers and media presenters – they all have work outs for their mouth muscles. Try these tongue twisters and see how they affect the muscles around your mouth.

She sells seashells on the seashore
Around the rugged rock the ragged rascal ran
The Leith police dismisseth us

Mike tried them, rather unwisely as he had just taken a mouthful of fish and nearly choked.

The Lion patted him on the back and then continued.

"Once you have control of your breathing and your articulation, you can then continue to think about where to put the emphasis in each sentence. This adds colour, texture and can even change the meaning.

"For example, if the waitress had said 'You *can* come back anytime' it might imply that we had previously been banned from this place.

"Now take this sentence:

I never said you were a lousy presenter

We can change the meaning eight times, simply by putting the emphasis onto different words."

Misha worked it through in her head.

"Got it! But it's scary the number of different ways it could be taken."

"Exactly. And that brings us neatly onto *the power of language*."

"You mean it's not what you say but the way that you say it?" said Mike.

"By and large, yes." replied the Lion. "Look, personal success relies largely on your ability to communicate. The way you say something is at least as important as what you say and often can have more impact than the actual words themselves. You need to engage the hearts and minds of your listeners if you are to influence them – and that goes for one-to-one conversations as well as for presentations.

"Skilled communicators use language in a way that creates a climate of trust and understanding. The difference that makes some people more successful than others is their instinctive ability to adapt their language to match that of the people to whom they are speaking.

Use of language

"Powerful communicators use language that is rich in all the senses – sight, sound, feel, taste and smell. We all use different sensing systems when processing language and usually we will have one or two preferences.

"Creative writing courses incorporate these ideas into their training," he continued. "By involving all the senses you have a chance of appealing to the largest possible group.

"By the same token, if you have two people who only use one sense when trying to communicate with one another and they are not using the same sense then they are likely to have difficulties at some stage.

"For example, if I am a visual communicator then I learn through seeing and having scenes described to me to create pictures in my mind. However, if all you do is tell me how it feels, I will not necessarily understand or remember your message."

"And we can apply the same principle to delivering presentations?" asked Misha.

"Right on! The same principle applies to any presentation. The emphasis is not simply on what you want to present, but on presenting the information in a way that will make the audience more receptive. Verbal descriptions may be an effective way of getting the audience to understand, but it may not be the best way of getting them interested. Just using one means of communication can become boring quite quickly.

"Presentations are like meals – they require variety. As the audience's role is basically passive – you are communicating one way to them – it is vital that you make the presentation more than just you and your words."

"So how would you sum all of that up?" asked Misha. "It sounds like a big subject."

"It is," the Lion agreed. "But in summary it is an attitude and a belief; our words must match our body language and you must believe your message.

"You must practise the colourful and emphatic use of language. For example, you could take a number of different and varied topics and practise how to get the message across about them in the most effective way using every technique to make the description vivid."

Mike was intrigued.

"Can you give us some examples?" he asked.

"How about practising some of the following:

Telling someone by telephone about your holiday while you are looking at the photos

Or

Describing a famous picture to a friend

Or

Talking about a television wine tasting programme

Or

Explaining a business procedure without having the right documents in front of you

Perhaps even...

Describing a bad smell.

"To develop your ability to change your voice, you can tell the story of Jack and Jill a number of times. Firstly in a boring style, then passionate, sexy, aggressive, calm, sad, happy, grating and then in a reflective style. I practice on my cubs, they think it is really fun and love guessing which style I am using."

"Hey, that sounds fun," exclaimed Mike. "I'm going to try the one about my holidays. Did you know, Misha that I once had a holiday in Tierra del Fuego, the ice flows there were..."

"Enough! Enough!" roared the Lion. "The sun is setting and if I don't get home in time for the hunt my wife will kill me, so we must press on."

"Can I ask a question?" said Misha. "How do you tell stories or use metaphors in your presentations?"

"You need to use all your verbal and non-verbal skills and tell the story as if you are really living it," said the Lion.

He started describing a list of simple guidelines:

Telling stories and metaphors

- Exaggeration really brings a story alive. It's the art of highlighting the point, but without telling a lie.

- Repeat the main points, but don't go on and on. Expand them into vivid detail.

- Rapport between the teller and the listener is vital; your story needs to fit to your audience.

- If you use humour, it needs to be appropriate and shared. If you offend half the audience in the first two minutes, you may never recover.

- Paint vivid pictures using multi-sensory language. Metaphors actually help you make sense of complex things. Remember a picture paints 1000 words.

- Don't be afraid of emotion, get into the emotion yourself and tell people what you were feeling if it helps you make impact. Present from the heart not the mind, be yourself and show your passion.

- Universal experiences are also a great way of creating rapport and a shared understanding with the audience. If 75 per cent or more of your audience have experienced what you describe you are on to a winner. For example learning to ride a bicycle, your first day at school or your first driving lesson. What experiences have your audiences known that could be included in your presentation? The audience will feel far more comfortable with you as they will feel you are like them and they can relate to you.

"Let's move on to talk about the non-verbal side of communication during your presentation."

The waitress arrived and asked what they would like for their dessert. The Lion looked wistfully at the space recently left by the gazelles, but settled for ordering coffee for three. His focus then turned to Misha who was fluffing up her feathers and holding her wings out at a forty five degree angle to cool herself down.

"Preening yourself or practising your non-verbal communication?" he asked.

7
Delivering the Presentation – The Body

Coffee arrived and Misha was keen to press on, which meant the conundrum of just how the penguins were going to drink their coffee without a straw or the like remained unanswered.

"Non-verbal communication? Now that sounds exciting," she exclaimed and flapped her wings in anticipation. This solved the whole coffee dilemma as both the penguins' cups were sent crashing onto the floor.

The waitress, who had developed a serious crush on the Lion, cleared the mess up without complaint.

"You're right, this is exciting but it's also where many presenters let themselves down," the Lion replied. "The non-verbal side of communication is vital as well over 55% of the real meaning behind the actual words you use is transmitted by what you do with your body. And therein lie the traps. For example, when giving a presentation, most penguins don't know what to do with their wings."

The body – what not to do

"Let's look at some of the more obvious ways in which you can go wrong. Firstly there is the CAGED TIGER. This is where the presenter paces up and down on the stage from one side to the other communicating restlessness and unease to all concerned. You must learn to stay in one place and only move when you have a clear purpose and even then make it a conscious, deliberate movement when you do.

"Then there is the FIG LEAF. Here the presenter stands with both paws clasped in front of his or her private parts. It makes you look like a footballer in the wall in front of a

65

free kick – or worse. Don't do it – use your paws to make gestures that add meaning and colour to your presentation and also to help you to keep in control."

"Sounds interesting," said Mike. "How do you do that?"

"We'll come onto that in a minute," said the Lion. "But first let's dispose of the traps. For example, some animals think that if they keep their paws in their pockets they can avoid some of the more obvious traps – the trouble is that you can look too casual or even become the COIN JINGLER."

Mike and Misha exchanged glances. They were both guilty of this.

"But perhaps being a coin jingler is better than being a PAW WRINGER," said the Lion. "When you stand there wringing your paws, your obvious worry quickly transmits itself to the audience and everybody ends up uncomfortable."

"But these are all negatives – surely there must be some positive uses of body language?" interrupted Mike, pointing at the Lion with his right wingtip.

"Indeed there are," said the Lion. "But POINTING directly at people is not one of them. The message transmitted seems to say '*It's your fault*' or '*It's down to you*'.

"This puts the other person onto the defensive – or worse, invites a counter-attack!"

The body – what to do

"The POINT is an effective communication technique though. You use it only once in the presentation to make your main point. You point above the audience's head and repeat the phrase or key point of your presentation. This emphasises both verbally and non-verbally the key message or point.

"Now let's look at some of the other more positive gestures and uses of body language."

The Lion finished his coffee, put down his cup, held both paws out, palms downward and moved then gently in a downwards direction.

"This is called THE WAY IT IS," he said. "The unspoken message is: '*this is true*.' It's assertive without being aggressive and helps you drive home a point."

"But supposing someone is being rather aggressive to you and you want to defuse it," asked Misha.

In reply, the Lion held up both paws, palms up and moved them slightly upwards. "What message do you think this gives?" he said.

"It looks like '*I'm being open with you*' or '*I'm aiming to please you, although not to give in to you*'. It can be used to ask the audience to participate or ask questions," answered a rather inspired Mike.

"Exactly. Now see if you can interpret this one." The Lion folded his arms in front of him and stroked his massive chin with one paw.

"It looks very intellectual and authoritative," said Misha. "It seems to say '*I'm the authority on this, here are the facts*', or perhaps '*I'm reasonable, logical and sensible*'."

"Quite," said the Lion. "We call that pose THE THINKER. It helps you exert what I call *intellectual command*. Try it, even if you don't think you've got intellectual command – the audience won't know. It can also buy you time if you do not know the answer to a question asked of you. Giving you time to think and answer in a thoughtful manner."

"I like this. There's more to it than I thought," said Mike. "Any others we should know about?"

"There are many, many others I could swamp you with so I'll just give you one other important one. This is THE JOKER. This is when the arms are asymmetrical; one pointing up and

the other down. This gives the message: 'I don't know' or 'it is not my fault'. It is often used when you say something you wished you had not, or when you use humour and it is the audience's cue to laugh."

"Are there any other uses for non-verbal techniques?" asked Misha.

"You learn to use them almost instinctively the more you practise and the more you present," replied the Lion. "But I will give you a couple of examples, one is about CONTROLLING ENERGY, the other is about CONTROLLING QUESTIONS."

"Energy, I've got no problems with that," said Mike.

"I've got bags of nervous energy, does that count?" Misha added.

The Lion groaned, partly at the penguins' ignorance and partly because the hunt was getting ever-closer and he knew as well as any that hell has no fury like a lioness scorned.

"Look, I'm talking about the energy of others as well as your own. Haven't you ever sat through a presentation where the whole room seems drained of energy?"

They nodded.

"And wasn't it grim – especially for the presenter?"

They both nodded more emphatically and the Lion continued.

Controlling energy

"You can send out energy through your eyes, your smile and even through the use of your limbs. If the audience seems to have little vitality, you may well have to fuel them with it yourself. If you are passionate about your subject it is likely your audience will be too.

"Your body has a natural centre which is about three inches below the navel. When your energy and attention rests in this centre you look and feel confident and ready for action.

"You need to learn how to 'ground' yourself; it helps you centre yourself. For example, when you stand let the ground 'support' you by letting your weight drop towards your feet. Concentrate on keeping your ankle, knee and hip joints soft. Or when sitting, let the chair support you, let the weight drop into your buttocks and feet, again keeping the ankle, knee and hip joints soft. This helps you look and feel relaxed, confident and in control."

"Is that better?" asked the Lion.

"Yes," said Misha. "But it's not easy."

"I never said it was easy – but I am saying it's important."

Both nodded again.

"Good. Now let's get on to answering questions."

Controlling questions

"Oh good! Answering questions worries me," said Misha.

"Well it shouldn't," said the Lion. "Questions are seldom hostile – except if you are a politician. They normally indicate that the audience are interested and that they want to know more. Animals seldom ask them to catch you out or show you up. However, when you are making a presentation, you want to be the one in control and you might well indicate when you are prepared to answer questions."

"And how do you do that?" asked Mike.

"Simple. You go to the QUESTION SPOT."

"The question spot?! What on earth are you talking about?" chorused the penguins.

"When you are prepared to answer questions, move deliberately to another part of the room or platform. Use your wings palm upwards and ask the audience are there any questions? The aim is to set up this spot to allow the audience to know when to ask questions and when to stop. If you ask the audience if there are any questions but they are not forthcoming, in a light-hearted fashion say '*come on this is the audience participation part of the presentation*' and nearly always a helpful soul will ask an appropriate question. The spoken and unspoken message is that '*when I am here I am happy to answer questions*'."

"And when you don't want to answer any more questions do you just move back to where you were before?" asked Misha.

"Exactly. The unspoken message is very powerful. You control when the questions come. As you will feel more relaxed about answering questions you will find that your answers are quite conversational and help create a more relaxed atmosphere."

"And is that finally all we need to know about giving presentations?" Mike and Misha said simultaneously as both were eager to feel that everything had been covered.

The Lion smiled.

"There is always something new to learn, but I've given you quite a lot to think about and it is getting late. It's been a long day for all of us."

A grateful Mike settled the bill and then turned to the Lion. "I think I can get this on expenses but is there anything else we really need to know before we go?"

"Maybe a couple of points but I'll go through them in the car park. Come on."

Out in the car park the sun was setting and the traffic was finally easing. A newspaper fluttered past them proclaiming that the reason for the earlier traffic chaos was that a group of sloth train drivers were on strike, demanding to do even less hours than they already did. Why anyone recruited sloths at all was one of the great mysteries of the animal world.

The Lion looked across at Mike and Misha.

"No more horses, no more bulldogs," he said. "Just one tired

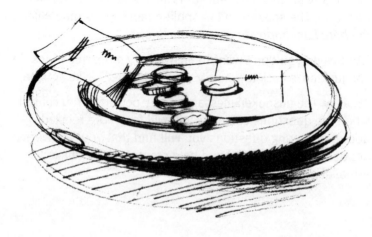

consultant Lion and a couple of young executive Penguins who hopefully have learnt something about presentations."

"You did say there were a couple of other things we needed to know," prompted Misha hopefully.

"Well not much. But, for example; how do you know if your presentation has been successful?"

"Rapturous applause?" inquired Mike.

"Perhaps – but even more significant is if people are still talking about it in the tea break or the day afterwards. That's when you know you've really scored!"

"So how do you build on your success?" asked Misha.

"For that we go back to the original purpose of the presentation. What did I define a presentation as earlier?"

Mike thought hard.

"An act of verbal persuasion; something you want people to say 'yes' to?"

The Lion grinned broadly and for a moment Misha remembered what big teeth he had.

"You've got it! That's the acid test. After that you must take whatever follow up action is necessary, whether it's to do with selling, going for that promotion or anything else. Strike while the iron is hot!"

Mike stuck out his flipper for the Lion to shake.

"I must say, you've taught me a lot," he said. "And we must let you go home"

"Before I do," said the Lion, "let me tell you one more thing. The key is **self-belief**. We were all made to communicate and we can all be better at communicating and presenting than in our wildest imaginations – if only we would let ourselves be so.

"So go on – give yourselves permission. If you believe you

can, you will be alright." He climbed into his car and leant out of the window.

"I'll be back for the next assessment centre in six months," he said. "I'll break a confidence and tell you that you are both destined to be on it. Go for it. You are both so nearly there.

"Just imagine and visualise you are both fifteen minutes after the successful completion of the presentation section of the assessment centre in six months time. Turn and look back to now."

Mike and Misha complied and immediately squawked in amazement – 'wow'. The anxiety had gone their emotions were flat and balanced.

"How does that work?" asked Mike, but the Lion just smiled knowingly.

"Believe in yourselves when you give those presentations – and remember what you have learnt and argued about this evening."

His car roared off into the darkness and Mike and Misha turned up their feathers to the wind. After bidding each other a somewhat pensive good night they got into their own cars.

With a small shiver, she wound up the window and followed Mike onto the highway. Fortunately the exit to Iceflow 12 was not far.

epilogue

Six months later and success

Misha stood by her window with the dreaded letter in her flipper. She willed herself to open it but it was taking time – the spirit was willing but the blubber was weak. As she started to tear the envelope she sensed a presence in her office and she looked up and saw Mike standing in the doorway.

"I hardly dare open it," he said. This was not the brash, loud Mike of six months ago but a more pensive, thoughtful penguin.

"Oh Mike, don't be such a baby!" said Misha. "Look, let's open them together... one...two...three..."

They both tore open their envelopes at the same time using their wings like paper knives.

"*Made it,*" shouted both penguins in delight and the next minute they were embracing with joy.

They disengaged and Misha quickly re-arranged her feathers and looked out of the window in embarrassment.

Stalking across the car park, with the sun setting on a fine evening was a large figure – the Lion.

"He really helped us," said Misha. "He may have scolded us and teased us, but he really helped us. I tried doing everything he said and it made it all so much easier."

"And *successful*," added Mike. "I suppose that if we rushed out now we could catch him and thank him."

"Yes, I suppose we could."

"But on the other hand, we might then get stuck with him for another evening of coaching and lecturing. There is an alternative..."

"Which is?" Misha's heart fluttered.

"That we each write him a letter of thanks but go out and celebrate, just the two of us together. I know of a great fish restaurant – fresh krill fish and squid just like from back home. What do you say?"

"Are you presenting the idea to me? Are you looking for a 'yes'?"

He winked. "Guess so..."

"Well who am I to say no?" she smiled.

The evening sun shone warmly on them as they waddled happily flipper in flipper into the car park. And unseen from his car, the Lion spied them. In the last six months Mike and Misha had shown great resilience and had put their learning into practice and it had paid off.

He felt a swell of pride in his manly chest and his massive teeth glinted as he smiled to himself. Then he remembered he had a pride of his own and if he didn't get back for the hunt then his wife would never forgive him.

"There are two kinds of penguins in the Antarctic, the white ones coming towards you and the black ones going away from you."

Anonymous